Another Attempt at Rescue

Another Attempt at Rescue

M. L. Smoker

Hanging Loose Press
Brooklyn, New York

Published by Hanging Loose Press, 231 Wyckoff Street, Brooklyn, NY 11217-2208. All rights reserved. No part of this book may be reproduced without the publisher's written permission, except for brief quotations in reviews.

www.hangingloosepress.com

Hanging Loose Press thanks the Literature Program of New York State Council on the arts for a grant in support of the publication of this book.

Printed in the United States of America
10 9 8 7 6 5 4 3 2

Cover painting by William Standing. See note on page 7.
Cover design by Pamela Flint

Shenandoah (Native American Poetry feature issue), ed. R. T. Smith, "Letter to Richard Hugo December 11, 2002"
Many Mountains Moving, "From the River's Edge"
Present/Tense: Poets in the World, ed. Mark Pawlak, "Another Attempt at Rescue"
Hanging Loose, "Migratory," "Intertribal." "From a Tin Box," "Seven Days Is Never Enough," The Necessary Bullet," "Can You Feel the Native American in Me" and "Venom"
Camas, "With/out"
South Dakota Review (Native American Writers), "lies lies lies"

Library of Congress Cataloging-in-Publication Data available on request

ISBN 1-931236-51-8 (paper)
ISBN 1-931236-52-6 (cloth)

 Produced at The Print Center, Inc. 225 Varick St., New York, NY 10014, a non-profit facility for literary and arts-related publications. (212) 206-8465

I am lost; I am looking for you
who can help me walk this thin line
between the breathing
and the dead....

Give me back my language
and build a house
Inside it.

A house for the dead
who are not dead.

from "We Must Call a Meeting"
—*Joy Harjo*

Art Credit

"Medicine Lodge, Fort Peck Reservation, Montana"
painted by William Standing in 1929

Pictured are (standing in back, left to right)
Moses White Horse, Iron Horn, Blue Cloud, James
Garfield, Pointing Iron, Tom Standing, Fire Moon,
Stonewall Jackson, Sib Fire Moon and Sophie Hamilton

(sitting left to right) Chinoop, Pipe, and Driver

(singers, left to right) Medicine Boy, Iron Leggins,
White Shield, Moses Crazy Bull, Four Star, Four Eagle,
Shy Face (back only) and Eagle Feather (back only)

(Lodge leader) Blue Horn

(Lodge candidate) White Wolf

Painting on loan to the Museum of the Rockies, from
the Peter Krudde family

Table of Contents

For my mother—*Ina je*

There are stories to be let loose with comb and water.
We gather these up again on shoulders and around waists
where they endure. This begins but does not end here:
we know only this route home.

.

Letter to Richard Hugo (1)

Dick: The reservoir on my end of the state is great for fishing. Some of the banks are tall and jagged, others are more patient, taking their time as they slope into rocky beaches. If you were the kind of fisherman I imagine, then you might have considered it a great place to cast from. My family has gone up there ever since the water on the Mni Shoshe was dammed off. My grandparents put on their moccasins and beadwork and danced for FDR when he rode the train out to see the finishing touches of this great industrial project. I haven't yet decided if this is something I wish to be proud of. Maybe this summer I'll spend more time up there, on the edge of a lake that was never meant to be a lake, and form an actual opinion. Maybe too I'll write you again. But you have probably already figured as much. I almost thought of not returning to finish the writing program you began with your own severe desire for language. But I did. And now I'm at the end. Already though, I'll admit to you, I'm thinking of home. I have been this whole time.

Blood and Body

From the River's Edge

Is it poetry to say that each time I cross over a certain bridge on the Yellowstone, I remember the way green vinyl felt on the back of my legs instead of how my own mother's feet, stiff from death, felt in my hands? I did not know that a poet could feel words rising from drops of sweat around her knees. Or that what my palms pressed against was only silence. Can a poet speak of a second version of her mother? The one who lives in a silent cave where she allows no visitors, gives no interviews. Her memoir is being written there by a shadow seven feet tall that can hold no pen or pencil, both hands missing. My living mother dreams of new waters that have no adequate translation.

The Necessary Bullet

[begin excited, anticipatory voice]
surely this is the route, the very route

[lose excited, anticipatory voice]
...we never once moved across. in how
many ways can we make this argument?

Asia is the blanket flashed across eyelids
the final scene unwinding, crumbling
against black edges.

[movie set make-up trailer, artist applies
heavy bronzer with care]
we are our own proof.

our language, July's mosquitoes, a man
with medicine all within three-four-five
dimensions as frozen waters subside.
it was the shape of our unspoken names
that etched out badlands and red rock plateau.

[university library, child seated among
high book stacks]
we will not ask again—do not use myth or legend.

another antelope crests the hills to the north
of a town remembered for the slaughter of wolves,
wolves stacked high beside train tracks—*you build*

such strange monuments to yourselves
she says to the view.

[archaeology lab, expert explains
the value of carbon dating]
there is no other way to take these things.

it is dark, there are train tracks to the east
under ice. men touch down palms to the cold
each knowing the others are thinking
this is science, most holy of holies.

can you hear the sound of old women clacking
their old tongues to the roofs
of their mouths in the dust?
this is prophecy so never
ask the Indian whether she'd take
the million dollars or the match.
gasoline is on the shelf in all our houses.

Seven Days Is Never Enough

monday
a dazzle of Christmas lights on seventh street
my mother's image
tattooed with the precision of a shaky
hand upon my back
reds on greens on yellows
a fusion that seems to say:
someone still lives here—don't
even think of knocking

tuesday
when I throw handfuls of salt
over my naked shoulder they become
a swarm of bees
which do you prefer
they ask:
the taste of sweaty skin
or a perfect bite of honeycomb?
the freckled boy next door
tells me i should never talk to strangers
he plays cowboys and Indians
bang bang

wednesday
my nephew storms into the room
he craves more than pepsi these days
so i hand him a seven-up
but he says i don't have cable
or a satellite like grandma

so we drive down to the river
and guess what belongs to who
as the trash floats by

thursday
maybe i'm back home
caught in a february blizzard
icicles frozen black from the stain
of glossy prayers that our dead
look away from
i smack my jaw
down hard
on the perfect
edge of a concrete sidewalk

friday
tano yudabish
"the day they don't eat meat"
lets all go out and slaughter something
the fattest animal
running across highway 2
a celebration, yes a celebration
of our own lovely carcass
rotting slowly on the bone
i smile for the cameras
a sweaty dollar bill feels good in my palm

saturday
the miniature man
comes to my side at night
your mattress is too tall he says
i dream of golden threads

tied throughout my golden hair
then tremble when the mirror
laughs among fluorescent lights
who would ever guess
these confused blood cells
curse and curse throughout the night

sunday
the battery in my watch slows
but i do not remember anymore
how to go outside
the door is an abyss
filled with coyotes
that know too many songs
my grandfather used to sing
only this time the words are backwards
where i come from
everyone knows
what that means

monday
someone slaps me hard across the face
i don't give a fuck if you
ever know what this is like
because this is ours, all ours
my cries combust into purple flames
and the smoke alarm sets its wail
alongside mine
a perfect harmony
always makes my hair tingle

tuesday
there is a certain shadow

that says it knows me
so i call my sister
because maybe she remembers
but the line is dead
should i ask what the lesson
is here
should i roll on the ground
for the secret message
that says
your life will never change
your life will never change

Lies Lies Lies

Tricky one: is it up or down / *don't talk to me because I am never lonely* / wheat fields turn silver against fierce winter skies / I howl at slivers of the moon pale as the skin on the soles of my feet / he asks me to dance again / I say you must give me another year / *don't invite me in because my belly is always full* / turquoise dreams are swallowed by glaciers the size of ten thousand buffalo / trains rattle on empty tracks as my brothers too seek any shelter / *if you come looking I'll say no one is home* / you laugh, Heyoka / living in two ways is never easy / maybe things will be different this time and you will speak the truth / say if it is danger or safety sitting at my feet.

Migratory

*"We don't really know it, but we sense it: there is a sister
ship to our life which takes a totally different route."*
                              —Tomas Transtromer

What if there is a catch? Or some sleight of hand
we should pretend to not see. Because the shadow
can be so near the truth.
I am hiding my mouth, again telling myself
questions are always such a mess. (And so
are mirrors for that matter.)
          I am not trying to be vague; I am trying to not
              mention "sister." Again the only thing we
              know for certain is a
setting apart.
          This is why I never visit oceans
          (and do leave things out).

I am unsure of this strange current of air moving so close
to another self. And speaking of birds
what is it they say exactly when the V pattern is broken?
This memory is not my sister and still this could
          be her name
if I allowed her to have one—
my unnamed likeness, who beads moccasins, speaks
          Assiniboine effortlessly.
How does one make amends
or know for certain who was at fault?
I might consider abandoning this place,
or any other. If only
we could each be granted one trial run.
We might be left to discover the sound
of contradiction in those wings.

Subsurface

Any map is confusing by design, useless. The few
remaining antelope taste ruin in the watershed long
before anyone thinks of eggshells fractured in the boiling
pan. We are bound to such places, ankle to barbed wire,
wrist to the halo of sky moving farther and farther
north. (No one remembers when they last saw the
preacher and his wife who clung to the wire cutters with
abalone knuckles.) How can we rest when all night long,
just a few miles toward the border, an invisible god's
hand keeps the iron hammers going, violent birds
snatching up the last of the liquid grain. Jaws clench in
sleep as the Morse code of machine taps sets the clocks
to an hour when our tongues have vanished and we
must beg with our eyes for another drop. Men we have
never seen before, their fingertips marked permanently
by spoiled silver ink, wait patiently as we grow new arms
and reach for their pens again.

With/Out

For Claire Hibbs

These days I have begun to tell myself *do not think
of north, do not think of rivers.* Today it is *do not
talk of autumn.* The leaves on my neighbor's oak
have let go. The wind is serious as it sets off
these small tornados. Small, yellow tornados circling
my house, keeping this quiet in. If I could go back
I would remove even yellow.

Each solitary larch tree branding itself against a forest
quickly gathering for winter is too much.
I would ask my friend if she saw the one half-covered
in black moss. It was near dying and still the branches
facing east held on. She would say *no one
should have to choose* and then I could easily forget.
These are favors I must remember to thank her for.

A light fixture in this small room is ornamented with
gold stalks trapped in a moment of wind.
Must I resist here too? Can the stalks speak
for themselves or break free?
Should I say *no northern fields, no distance
of rivers, no mother*—for all our sakes?
(And if one removes *mother* then must *father*
also be taken away?) This could go on for some time.

Several Poems for the Non-Indian in Me

"And you remember who killed who.
For this you want amnesty."
　　　　　　　　　　　—Linda Hogan

"Collaborate: v. 1) to work together, or, *2) to help the enemy."*

to work together
She asks only that you forget
all of the usual questions like
where are you from?
or when will you return?

to help the enemy
As a young girl she tried the violin
forcing her fingers onto the neck—
stiff motion of bow upon string.
Hands would grow tired, not hold
true to form. She had not yet learned
to blame their unruliness on the past.

to help the enemy
She casts language about, thinking herself
in control.
Her contention—that words are wild but willing—
often degenerates into quite
an uncivilized competition.
This causes some confusion
as she is unable to remember
the most accurate truth:
a) she might have learned indifference, to forget

the stories she never heard one grandma
speak of. b) she listened to each story, careful
to set them down in true Boaz form.

to work together, to help the enemy
Her father calls to say how much
he misses her. She does not pick up.
She blames him for Removal
and for the battle scenes she relives.
"The fog was not so heavy this winter.
You should see how the orchard is growing,
green shoots above my head."
She cares little, if any, for such mobility.

to help the enemy
Commands are given, portions further split.
Her new home, she finds,
is built on tilted land.

to work together, to help the enemy
Planes circle overhead like angels.
Water runs beneath the crack
of a door memory cannot unlock.
She fails to see how words,
an instrument of reinvention,
might belong to that flood.
She tries.

Territorial

as the river drafts a new course
the bank grows steeper
more the antagonist

(and these stories we are born into
they are just as conflicted—my own
and my mother's)

we do not know how to witness
this change and so what do we make
of the silt and the slip

what do we make
of the insufferable heat wave
she is born within

even the insects so rampant
and wild in september
hold themselves

to small pockets of earth
i too invent winter
callous and frozen shut

in the nearly broke-down
car she opens the door
to the highway and asks

why—not of the storm
but of me these
arrivals

are they false
record or the stubborn
tangling of leaves

will i grow to be as unforgiving
let them say *no you were born
into a rain-filled month* say *no you were*

born here—look again
the river is turning back
stems in their moment of breaking

Tatogana

Yes, this year has been hard on all of us. The antelope have even taken to crossing the lake, maybe attempting an instinctual, yet impossible move to warmer climates. Just last week the ice gave way and more than eighty were lost to the lake's cold water, limbs and hooves torn from the fight to break free. Those who had been spared stood looking on in both misery and curiosity. When the rescue team and boats arrived, they rushed to pull as many as possible to safety. Then in so short a time the only work left was loading heavy carcasses and hauling them to land. Quickly, as it does this time of year, evening came and the crews moved toward their vehicles, the bloated antelope piled in the beds of their pickups. Only when the engines started did the animals left on the lake's dark shore stir, their gaunt faces lingering and unafraid in the red glow of taillights moving back toward town.

So Far, So Long

Here the cold is much different. With each difficult, stiff breath we are reminded of one heartbreak after another. The man makes his way from the train station, headlong into these conditions and a merciless wind. He still knows how to get wherever he needs to go but one can never be fully sure of the memory of what's been left behind and the only thing he knows to do with any certainty is to light another cigarette. He could be returning from the worn-out streets of Minneapolis or Denver, only to find his hometown a much lonelier place than he'd remembered it. Maybe with each inhale of tobacco smoke he conducts his own private ceremony, taking account of time between here and there, asking if he should get back on. Or what if he admits that it was only a matter of time and that winter is always the most forgiving time of year.

Casualties

*"...linguistic diversity also forms a system necessary
to our survival as human beings."*

—Michael Krauss

The sun has broken through.
Breaking through,
this sun—but still
today my words   are dying out.

Still as I tell of   stillness
of a very word
as ( )   as it leaves this world.

*My grandmother was told that the only way to survive was
to forget.*

Where   were you?
     Where were
you? Speaking of myself,
for   my own neglect: too often
I was nowhere to be found.
     I will not lie.
        I heard the ruin in each Assiniboine voice.
I ignored them
all. On

     the vanishing, I have been
mute. I have risked
a great deal.
Hold   me   accountable

because I have not done my part
     to stay alive.

As a child I did not hear the words often enough to recognize
what I was losing.
      There are a great many parts of my own
body that are gone:

where hands
belong there is   one lost syllable.
And how a tooth might sound—
its absence
     a falling.

Sound   is so frail a thing.

(   )   hold me responsible,
in light   of failure
     I have let go   of one too many.

I have never known where or how
     to begin.

Untitled

But on a train between Browning and Izaak Walton Inn,
perhaps as some form of penance,
I witnessed a grizzly tear into a fallen tree trunk
with muscle, claw and all the force
of her own body. (She too
was seeking a form of sustenance.)

I find that certain words arrive first:
in the woods heavy with near darkness
she could only be known by one name—*wakan sija.*
As in instinct: "this bad holy thing."

In the passage that exists between word
and thought
I have been forced
to learn a great deal of the collapse
of one language upon another.
I offer up many explanations for this
too-often conflicted tongue, never
arriving at any shape of reconciliation.

If forgiveness were molded between my hands
what might it resemble?

And why not?
Haven't millions prayed for the transubstantiation?
I am asking for this same miracle,
the blood and body of the only language
I want to be known by.

Grandfather Poem

His words are the ones no longer spoken, rising instead
from the steam in a kettle on the blackened wood stove.
He is almost blind but pours the cups with a steady hand:
"Coffee for this granddaughter, nighttime is on her mind."

Oyade wihamna. Hageji.
     Iyuha ezhedu wihamnabi.
        Oyade wihamna.

I pack fresh tobacco, begin the long walk.
Winds cut and cross over ravine, then plateau and ravine
     again.
I enter a door which faces south and I do not feel ashamed
for entering this way. I think of a mother and father in sleep.
I know then of the distances we will devise,
navigate imperfectly.

Oyade wihamna. Hageji.
     Iyuha ezhedu wihamnabi.
        Oyade wihamna.

My grandfather and I sweep down through the yielding
     riverbed,
walk the quiet rushes of the Mni Shoshe, then move north,
to higher ground. He motions toward the ponies as they
     rise up
and release their tears, large drops the size of ripe apples.
They dance then, as my mother and father shift in sleep,
dreaming to the rhythm of horses' hooves.

Oyade wihamna. Hageji.
   Iyuha ezhedu wihamnabi.
      Oyade wihamna.

From a Tin Box

    In my uncle's old army chest the teeth of an elk rattle—a full-grown elk who gave up his life one November. The chest is standard issue, safe at the side of my uncle's bed. Every morning his toes touch down, four inches from the metal, from the strong ivory-tinted teeth that listen for this awakening. He smiles at this. He calls the teeth a shelter, a low ridge sprouting new grasses. My uncle opens the chest and gathers them into the shadow of his thick, cupped palms. He confides in them a dream from the night before, ever careful to listen for its meaning as the teeth click quietly together and sing.

Down to This

Venom

We are the kids outside the bingo hall. My brother is inside calling the numbers as they show their faces on the fluorescent Ping-Pong balls, my mother helps to serve Indian tacos to all the old people, my auntie plays with three cards and her own fierce luck that makes people wonder. We are all outside in June, charged by mosquitoes who aim for the spots we can't see—behind kneecaps, in the parts of our dark hair, on the edges of ear bone. We forget all about our boredom, the blood, and the bites when one of our cousins yells he's found a rattlesnake in the tall grasses around the corner. We all run to see it, to hear it, to get close enough to tell stories about it later in the summer. One of the older boys gathers his young courage and moves toward it with a stick. He realizes before the rest of us that all it is is the long shredded skin of a rattler that has moved on, probably down toward the river. He picks the discarded shell up with his knobby birch stick and then throws it high into the air. We all run and scream, afraid of poisons and pain. We cannot say enough about the poisons and pain.

Another Attempt at Rescue

March 20, 2003

The time is important here—not because this
has been a long winter or because it is my first
at home since childhood—but because there is so much
else to be unsure of. We are on the brink of an invasion.
At a time like this how is it that when I left only a week ago
there was three feet of snow on the ground,
and now there is none, not even a single patch
holding on in the shadow of the fence-line.
And to think I paid a cousin twenty dollars
to shovel the walk. He and two of his buddies,
still smelling of an all-nighter, arrived at 7 am
to begin their work. When I left them a while later
and noticed their ungloved hands, winter made me feel
selfish and unsure. This ground seems unsure
of itself for its own reasons

and we do not gauge enough of our lives
by changes in temperature.
When I first began to write poems
I was laying claim to battle.
It started with a death that I tried to say
was unjust, not because of the actual
dying, but because of what was left.
What time of year was that?
I have still not yet learned to write of war.
I have friends who speak out—as is necessary—
with subtle and unsubtle force.
But I am from *this* place and a great deal

has been going wrong for some time now.
The two young Indian boys who almost drowned
last night in the fast-rising creek near school
are casualties in any case.
There have been too many just like them
and I have no way to fix these things.

A friend from Boston wrote something to me last week
about not having the intelligence
to take as subject for his poems
anything other than his own life.
For a while now I have sensed this in my own mood:
This poem was never supposed to mention
itself, other writers, or me.
But I will not regret that those boys made it home,
or that the cousins used the money at the bar.
Still, there are no lights on this street.
Still, there is so much mud outside
that we carry it indoors with us.

Birthright

for Carl Lithander

We talked once of driving all the remote gravel
roads, writing from here and there, a little like Hugo,
though neither of us had read his poems yet. Today I am
wondering about those unwritten drafts. Could they
have predicted the severity of this drought, would they
have spoken to our own landscape, one of anger,
sympathy and remorse: You, the eventual heir to your
family's homestead; and me, an Indian woman who
leases her land to white men made up of the same storm
and grit and hunger as your grandfather. What if we had
found a message in verse written from some small
town?—*abandon this place.* Would we have listened and
turned the car east or south and left behind the land our
families have lived on for generations? But where could
we travel and not long for the ache of wind blowing over
open land? And how long could we have held ourselves
back, away from our need to feel claimed by a place we
can only, with our limited tongue, call home.

The Feed

Several of my cousins lean up against the house, taking long drags from the pack of Marlboros we share. We have always been this way—addicted and generous. A pow wow tape plays from inside the open garage where two old uncles are thinking to themselves in the safety of its shadows. Our aunties are in the kitchen, preparing the boiled meat and chokecherry soup and laughing about old jokes they still hang onto because these things are a matter of survival. Outside, we ask about who was driving around with who last night, where so-and-so got beat up, whose girlfriend left him for someone else. (But she'll go back to him, we all think to ourselves.) Aunties carry the full pots and pans to the picnic table, an uncle prays over our food in Assiniboine. We all want to forget that we don't understand this language, we spend lots of time trying to forget in different ways. No one notices that the wild turnips are still simmering in a pot on the stove.

Winter Again

Once I drove long winter hours alone, snow swirling
in drifts from one half of the covered plain
to the other. My mother was alive then
and I made my way toward the temptation of finally
getting things right between us.
No matter what size the storm outside
I drove on because I could not live with anything else.

When I arrived it was late and I crawled into the bed
next to her and somehow the distance
between our lives had made our breathing,
our hands, indistinguishable.
Now she has been gone for some time
and again I am searching for evidence
that we are more than just blood.

In summer there is the quiet of new leaves settling
and resettling upon one another
to remind me of how the fragile edges overlap.
But this time of year the trees are leafless and as I find
myself settling and resettling into the very place
she is still tied to, I think of creases
across our knuckles, the palm's winding rivers
reaching out toward the fingertips.

There is no easy explanation, no sudden burst of
I see now or *some things must remain lost,*
only the unwoven lifelines of two women.
I muddle through the fragments, none of which

can tell me why the reflected light from snow
outside my window seems like a better,
more perfect sort of light. Or why it is

I have gone to her grave only twice
since returning home for good.
After all, she is what brought me here.
But I am not clever enough to discern
those patterns she and I revolve around, let alone
why I have taken to ashing my cigarettes in a shell
from some unremembered ocean,
thinking of gods I fail to pray to.

Now would seem like an appropriate time, but all
I can consider are the formations of new frost
on the trees, just before midday strips
each thin branch bare again.

Forward & Reverse

There is an old sky-blue Dodge heading south as memory clings to bone of Continental Divide. No radio in the truck, the heat does not work, the girl is five years old but not shivering. She dreams that back in her home the water is spilling over from the tub, onto the wearied linoleum. She almost remembers the color of the bathmat her mother sits on, head in her hands. Back on the dimming highway a woman in the next car passes illegally on the right. She sees the girl's cheek pressed to the window in sleep and thinks of pumpkins cut from the vine.

Crosscurrent

for James Welch

The first harvest of wheat in flatlands
along the Milk startled me into thoughts of you
and this place we both remember and also forget as home.
Maybe it was the familiarity or maybe it was my own
need to ask if you have ever regretted leaving.
What bends, what gives?
And have you ever missed this wind?—it has now
grown warm with late summer, but soon
it will be as dangerous as the bobcat stalking calves
and pets just south of the river.
Men take out their dogs, a case of beer and wait
in their pickups for dawn, for a chance with their rifles.
They don't understand that she isn't going to make
any mistakes. With winter my need for an answer
grows more desperate and there are only four roads out.
One is the same the cat hunters drive with mannish glory
and return along, gun still oil-shined and unshot.
Another goes deeper into Assiniboine territory:
This is the one I should talk myself into taking next.
I haven't much traveled the third except to visit
a hospital where, after the first time,
my mother had refused chemotherapy.
And the last road you know as well as I do—
past the coral-painted Catholic church, its doors
long ago sealed shut to the mouth of Mission Canyon,
then south just a ways, to where the Rockies cut open
and forgive. There you and I are on the ascent.
After that, the arrival is what matters most.

Call It Instinct

for Rob Schlegel

Earlier today when I crossed the Rockies at MacDonald Pass
I realized how beautiful graffiti can appear on boxcars
moving carefully in this early winter.
Our friend's poems were lying on the truck's dashboard,
and I saw the word "fantastic," spelled there with a "c,"
talking about polished secrets,
and again later, crafted by a tagger in spray paint,
spelled "fantastik."

Each time I return to Missoula
it gets more and more difficult to leave for home.
This is not a betrayal of home:
It means I am resorting to standard forms of expression
for missing people and not knowing how
to finally arrive at (depart for) some other place.

I have been meaning to tell you that early
one morning on my drive to the school
I too saw a coyote, her matted fur whitened
for movement across this patchy, snowy plain.
She stood just a short distance off the highway
and I saw her eyes, just in that moment
of passing. I saw her eyes but I will tell
you nothing of their color: Call it instinct.

What are we native to? All along
I have said it was landscape and the language
wrought there according to wind and need.

But I have begun to change my opinion, not of where
and who I come from, but of how
we might establish a particular resonance:
As in coyotes and stones and the full
relationship between thought and deed.
The "fantastik" we all might choose—if given the chance—
to name ourselves over again.

Sparrow's Sleep

As a child she would trouble herself each bedtime over the hours. Her father, who built her a bed of five mattresses stacked one on top of the other, would say *you don't have to worry about those things.* But she could never fully believe him and she could never stop herself from counting, well into the night, anxious over the school nurse's admonition: *at least eight hours, healthy children need at least eight hours.* And she wanted to be like all of the other kids. She wanted a horse and her old house back and all of the family they had left behind in that small reservation town. It was soon after they left that she refused to sleep on any bed that had a frame lifting it from the ground—something about all that empty space being too much like the hours spent hovering over the road in their Dodge as they drove farther and farther away. An hour, then two, then sometimes three would pass and eventually her father would come to sit quietly in a chair in the corner of the room. Only then could she lose track of the restless addition and subtraction, of the distance between one place, one life and another.

Borrowing Blue

I'm not the painter here. I leave that to you, but blue
is the color of my father's camping cup, left tonight
on the Formica counter. This pen I am writing with.
And the beaded moccasins and belt I danced in
before my mother died.
My grandmother had made these for her as a child—
spelling out in blue beads on blue beads
each of our names, our collective history
in an invisible pattern only we would recognize.
Not the blue of Montana sky either,
not that at all, but the pulse of lake water lapping
at your ankles, the temperature rising
as a storm gathers on the plains.
The push and pull of forgiveness.
I'm already thinking of leaving again.
Did I tell you this? How can I speak of this wind,
how it has no color, no sense,
no guilt. It makes me feel even more lonely
than I would ever let on.
I'm guessing you figured this much already.
(We will never stop missing them, will we,
the parent each of us has lost.)
I'll be honest, I have no idea what I would see
in the paintings if I were to visit you.
I like to think there would be some kind of end
to the blue, a visual end to what is never
adequate: blue flame, blue bead, blue ovary,
blue lung. See how easily we fail?
How can we believe that our secrets are in good hands—

yours resting at the bottom of Flathead Lake, mine held
in a small leather suitcase beneath the stairs.
I have not worn those moccasins or that belt for over
six years now. We should both be ashamed.
Look at us. Look, as the grey fog
settles into your streets outside, how the near-white
canvases wait. You almost didn't notice again.
Just like I almost didn't notice the wind
dying down for evening.
So yes, let's call it Montana blue, the vanishing point:
Maybe this is the real reason I have never learned
to trust in color. How can you take back
the kind of blue you've been dreaming of—trust
it will make something unhappen—
if it is the same blue you're made of?

Intertribal

We dance to our clan song, wearing the red shawls from a cousin's give-away. We step carefully, shoulder to shoulder, hair dyed—last time all of us girls wanted to try black cherry. Still, dust from under the arbor turns our hair gray. We begin to look like our mothers. This makes old women resting in folding chairs grow nervous. They sit along the outskirts of the dance circle and whisper about us, this next group of Indian girls, all cousins, who come from Frazer. They know it will be us who stop their grandsons to talk after the pow wow. It will also be us who sing to them in the early morning hours, who hold them, who ask them to stay.

Can You Feel the Native American in Me

We pull into dirt driveway in Lara's blue Celica. The car came from her 18 money last year and it's got only one dent on the side from a white girl in Wolf Point who slammed the door of her boyfriend's Ford pick-up into the passenger side of Lara's then new car. Lara was pissed, got out to kick the girl's ass but they sped out of the Town Pump's parking lot too fast. That girl was scared. Lara came back to the car and we laughed at that dent, but most of all we laughed at that fear. Driveway to uncle's house, we're bumping Tupac, get out, step into sweat lodge. Got a sick auntie. Take in a towel, leave out hip-hop beat, add in hand drum. Our uncle forgives us this time for being late and we are more sorry for this than we were for quitting the basketball team or for getting pregnant last year.

One Year

and this—the corners of my mouth have grown dry,
accustomed to the cold temperatures and hard winter.
I flake off skin with my fingernails, nervous
about the indication of having been someplace
for too long. Too long for one war to carry on.
Certainly this, yet it hardly seems believable,
that it should all end up here, again with winter
not yet loosened, this creaking chair and still too close
to what we cannot reconcile.
No one tells us how long these things must remain,
how long I must remain—
So who can be surprised when we develop a nervous habit,
sleep fewer hours, talk to empty rooms?
It isn't as easy as saying *make do*
and there is only the indication of an early spring.
I have not adequately prepared, not thought enough
about what this might mean. (*Take up elsewhere now?*)
But the creeks and ditches are all at the point
of flowing over. And the fields, empty of wheat
for months yet, will not be able to hold back the swell.
Yes, everyone will be confined to their homes again
as roads and neighborhoods flood, animals drown.
What will I have then to speak about? What will remain
for anyone to say?—"too long
she was left to herself that way."
Or maybe I should listen to a friend, ask
fewer questions, believe a little more in what I know:
the days again, finally hanging on.

It Comes Down to This

The man who owned the only saddlery shop in town refused, until the day he died, to sell back my grandfather's grass dance regalia. When the shop owner was still alive, the wiry hairs on his knuckles stood on end each time a new wind blew down Main Street. Later he grew to call this "cancer" but I will always call it *he should have known better*. His wife, in some form of mourning, says she too won't sell us a single piece, even if we can prove with old photos of my grandfather that it was his. Instead she says we have to buy the whole shop, leather-crafting tools and all. (I heard it said once that her husband made her promise this on his deathbed, but who can say for sure.) Last month, on a below-zero midnight, the building next door burned to heaps of wreckage and ash, a brick wall separating the flames from a glass case that holds my family's heirloom. They called this "luck," that the whole block didn't go down too. I call it *what's ours is ours*.

Letter to Richard Hugo (2)

Dick: Once, in one of the small creeks that runs from Fort Peck Lake I saw a catfish, swimming upstream, trying to make it back to the shelter of a larger body of water. It was late summer and there wasn't enough of the creek to cover the top half of his fins. Still, he pushed down into the mud and kept on. I did not envy him. Nor did I devise some plan to help him make it back to safety. I'll let you draw your own conclusions about what type of person this makes me. And since we're on this track: I have a sister I haven't spoken to in years. And the language my relatives spoke while getting ready for the dam's inaugural ceremonies is close to extinction, but I have always made up something more important to do, rather than take the risk of saving it. I am still angry at times with my father because I long for the type of mother mine could never have been. I go on mourning her, even though a medicine person has told me it was time to let her go to the other side. I wonder if she is still close, or if years ago she ignored me and went on. I certainly didn't know that today—when I'm a week away from packing up, leaving Missoula for good, and making my way east for home—I would sit here in the purplish light of the first real snowfall of the year and write to you. I could go on, tell you about my poetry, about how much it's meant to spend time with Ripley, about the influence Jim has been. (Thank you for telling him to write what he knew. That allowed me to write what I know, twenty-five years later, from another rez a little farther down the road.) I'll just close by saying the salmon are plentiful, even if they begin their lives in a hatchery down below the dam. For the time being, I don't mind this as much, and I have an idea you wouldn't either. There's just something about the remissible wave of a cast which feels like the biggest commitment of all.